The Fox Who Sneezed

Can You Guess What Came Out?

Elle Valentina Dubois & Grampa Steve

Illustrations by Sarah Feragen

Paperback ISBN: 978-1-4787-9315-1
Hardback ISBN: 978-1-4787-9518-6

Illustrations By © 2018 Sarah K. Feragen. All rights reserved - used with permission.

PRINTED IN THE UNITED STATES OF AMERICA

Foreword

By Linda Ostrander, DMA, PhD, Author of *Journeys in the Land of Spirits* and *Between Mothers and Daughters*.

The Fox Who Sneezed is a delightful story created by Elle Valentina Dubois and Grampa Steve. The story employs familiar characters in new guises and situations, and successfully keeps the reader wondering how the plot will be resolved. I am amazed at the creativity and insight of the young author who, starting at age five, developed her awareness of characters and plot, and maintained her purpose over the past two years to complete this engaging book.

Grampa Steve is also to be commended for his persistence with the project, teaching what he learned in his storytelling classes, and translating it into the appropriate language and techniques for his young student. One can see that it is a labor of love.

The colorful, imaginative illustrations by Sarah Feragen and Philip Costa complement the story very well. From the frizzly-squiggly hair of the old man to the scary, hairy Fox, the characters come to life and will delight young readers.

Finally, I must comment on the surprising and sophisticated "secret" that underlies the plot—that allergies can be good! As one who suffers from allergies, I am beginning to look at them quite differently. They alert me to things that are not good for me and which I should avoid. Maybe the Fox will learn his lesson and no longer chase the Gingerbread boy!

Linda W. Ostrander, DMA, PhD.

Acknowledgments and Thank You(s)

Elle and I (Grampa) are grateful for everyone who has listened to every story, good or bad, that we tell and re-tell. And we are especially grateful to Elle's mom and dad for believing in Elle's ability and for creating the space in Elle's life to plan, organize, and create this book. To Grammy Susan, thanks for all the love and patience to listen to this story and other stories many times over so that the stories could mature. And thanks to Grammy for proofreading, too.

Thank you to Pop-Pop and Grandma for Elle's wonderful care as a toddler, and the encouragement for Elle to tell stories from the very beginning, when Elle said her very first sentence in their driveway at nine months old: "I WANT MOMMY!" Thank you to Ninnie and Dada for being so excited at any mention of the book, and for helping to create Elle's very cinematic aura. And a great big thank you to all those who listen at school or at home when Elle asks to tell her stories and develop her craft.

And from Grampa: To all of you who know that I'm stuck at nine years old – thank you for the space to be myself. And thank you to my beautiful and patient wife for listening, and listening, and listening...and for allowing the space in our lives for stories to grow. And special thanks to my mentors Ed Ostrander (who is alive in every story we tell) and his beautiful wife Linda Ostrander, who are a continuing inspiration in my life.

To Elle's mom and dad for sharing their beautiful children Elle and Dave (D3) so that our stories can together lift us to great, unexplored places to learn and grow. And to my sons Phil and Dave (and their wives Jess and Rory) for covering the "front door" while I continue my imagination work with their precious help.

Thanks to Phil for the Fox in our book too! And thank you to my grandchildren Cam and Chloe for encouraging, creating, and listening to stories that have helped shape us all. Keep going...keep going...keep going! Together with Elle and Dave, Cam and Chloe make up the "stinky brats" brigade which has given me my **raison d'être, as my journey goes from old to young, and younger still.**

To Elle, thank you for the many sparks your energy and imagination give off that ignite my stories and light the room when you are there.

Special BIG thanks from Elle to Sarah Feragen, the most imaginative artist ever, for the wonderful illustrations, which give life to the stories we tell.

Kudos to the team at Outskirts Press for their help in making my dream of shared growth through family storytelling a reality.

And finally our thanks to Linda Ostrander, author and mentor, for the Foreword to *The Fox Who Sneezed*. Linda, you are a lighthouse in the stormy seas of life. We cherish you!

A Message to Our Readers:

From Our Hearts to Yours:
The story behind writing *The Fox Who Sneezed*:

From Elle and Grampa:
Thank you for reading.
We'd like to share how this book came to be.

My Grampa told me that a long time ago, when months were moons, and mice were ooze, and dogs were dinner, he learned to tell stories from a storyteller named Ed. I think Ed was very smart, and very good at telling stories, and Grampa is too.

I've listened to the singing sounds, and imagined the faraway places, and seen the crazy characters of those stories since I was born. As anyone who knows me can say, those stories lit a "talking fire" in me. After hearing oodles of Grampa's stories, one day I decided to tell my own stories to Grampa. He liked my stories, and kept asking for more stories, and asked me if I'd like to write this story down.

The first draft was very incomplete and took us several hours. He wrote whatever I said into his computer as I spoke, without too much editing. I had to think of what the characters in the story looked like, where they were, and what they were doing. I also had to think of a message to share. We didn't really figure out the final plot and the message until we were about halfway done.

On the day we started (Jan 10th, 2016), we just started right in. I was five and I didn't know how to write, so Grampa wrote down what I said as

v

I told the story from my imagination. Each time we took a break from the story, which could be a day, a week, or a month, we'd restart by Grampa reading me everything we'd written so far. Then we'd think together about what the story was, what the characters were doing, and how to tell the story, and then we'd write some more.

We continued to work on the book whenever we had quiet time together. Sometimes I had to push Grampa to make time for us to write another chapter, because he was busy. Several times we changed the action in the book to better share the message. As we finish the book, I'm now seven years old. I can read and write now. So when we revise the story, I read the story instead of Grampa. It has taken us almost two years to finish, and we are very proud of the book. The book has made us very close.

Toward the end, to make our story more interactive with our audience, we added some chants and rhymes that are fun, and we hope you'll sing along with whoever reads the book. We hope you like the book as much as we do, and hope that you might write your own stories with your family someday. We'd love for you to tell us what you think, or ask questions through our special email for the book: TheFoxwhosneezed@gmail.com.

Table of Contents

Finding the Gingerbread House

Once upon a time, there was an old lady and an old man trying to find a Gingerbread House. They knew an important secret. They were going to tell the Gingerbread Boy the secret when they found him.

The old lady was a little bit plump, wearing an all-purple dress. Her hair was grey, stringy, and wet.

The old man was dressed in really tight blue pants, and he had grey glasses that helped him to see the dangers of the forest. His glasses were magical--they let him see high up to the sky and down into a person's heart. He got the glasses from Spotty, a friendly, magic Giraffe who had a long brown tongue. The old man's thick hair was made up into a squiggly, wiggly hairstyle. There was one very strange thing about him. Do you know what it was?

...He had a blue tongue.

The old couple searched all morning and into the afternoon. They had to go through the dark forest. It was very scary, because they had to watch out for the mean old Fox, who might try to eat them. Finally they found a Gingerbread House. The front was brown with pink gumdrop buttons for doorknobs, and shutters made out of chocolate. The roof was candy-striped. As they looked around in front of the candy house, they thought they were safe, but they weren't.

Sketch by Philip Costa—Colored by Elle Valentina Dubois at age six.

2

The Sneaky Fox

There was much evil in the forest – and the evil Fox was nearby. He was a mean Fox, orange, white, and black, with sharp teeth and sharp claws. If you ever saw that Fox, you would be scared to death.

And that wasn't the worst of it. There was a witch that was helping the Fox to steal young children (just like you).

The witch had both short and long hair. On the left side it was very short and blue in the most awful way.

The witch was two-sided, like some people you meet. The witch's left side had light-blue hair, which made her look really, really, nice. But the right side had bats clinging to her long, oily hair. Her clothes were purple with gold stars, tempting you to think she was good, but she was very, very bad. She flew on a magic broom that would take her wherever she wanted to go. The Fox ran after her at night but not in the day, because the broom was nocturnal, meaning the broom couldn't stand the sun at all – the same as the witch.

What is going on tonight?

Animals running left and right,

[Group says] Will we be *a snack tonight?*

The magic witch has taken flight,

Children hiding out of sight,

Oily hair with rat and bat,

Everyone should hide from that

Fox and bats are giving chase

Under the moon's bright, shining face

We hope the witch goes hungry tonight

Or it'll be a nasty sight.

Moon hides its face and travels low,

Morning light, and off they go.

3

The Accidental Mistake

Upon finding the Gingerbread House, the old couple excitedly knocked on the gingerbread door. Suddenly, the pink gumdrop doorknob quietly started to turn. Unexpectedly, the Fox came out of the house in disguise. His orange, white, and black fur was hidden in a gingerbread suit to make him look like he was part of the gingerbread family. His nasty nose and large teeth were hidden under a large black hood. The old couple asked to speak to the Gingerbread Boy.

But the Fox said in a fake Gingerbread Man voice, "The Gingerbread Boy isn't here. He's out playing with the Three Little Pigs. I'll help you find him."

The old couple thought something was wrong, but they didn't know what it was. They could feel something. Together they said in a whisper,

"Are we right?"

[Group says] Or are we wrong?

"His nose looks awfully long!"

4

Fox Is Up To No Good

Hoping for a good result, together the old couple and the Fox, who was disguised as the Gingerbread Man, went off to find the Three Little Pigs and the Gingerbread Boy.

What do you think the Fox was up to?

As the three of them reached the hill where the Three Little Pigs lived, something was very strange. All the animals were running away as fast as they could.

"Are we right?"

[Group says] Or are we wrong?

"His claws look awfully long!

Animals running left and right!"

[Group says] We might be *a snack tonight?*

Somehow the animals knew that the Fox was hiding in the Gingerbread Man's clothes. They could smell him. When the Three Little Pigs saw what was happening, they ran too. The old Fox couldn't help himself, as he jumped out of his fake clothes and chased the pigs into their house-- along with the Gingerbread Boy. That's when IT happened.

5

Bad News for the Three Little Pigs

The Three Little Pigs were trapped. The Fox drooled as he opened his mouth wide and ate the Three Little Pigs all at once in one big gulp--one...two...three. But he couldn't fit the Gingerbread Boy in his mouth. The Gingerbread Boy sat in the corner frozen as he watched his friends get eaten. *Oh, how awful*, the Gingerbread Boy thought. And then he said,

"Oh, NO! What can I do?

This must be wrong. This can't be right!"

[Group says] We might be a snack tonight!

"I must help my friends,

From Fox's stomach, into the air.

We really need a hero here!"

Before the Gingerbread Boy could finish his thoughts, the Fox leaped into the corner and grabbed the Gingerbread Boy by the neck and tried to take a bite. But instead, he sneezed the biggest sneeze ever, and out of his mouth burst the Three Little Pigs – one, two, three.

The Fox, looking really mad, grabbed the Gingerbread Boy again, but as he tried to eat him, he sneezed a second, giant sneeze.

6

The Escape

The Fox's second sneeze was so big that the air from his sneeze pushed the Three Little Pigs AND the Gingerbread Boy right out of the Three Little Pigs' house. The Three Little Pigs ran as fast as they could, but not as fast as the Gingerbread Boy. He ran faster than a kangaroo. Faster than a rabbit, too. He was really scared. The angry Fox looked everywhere, but couldn't catch any one of them.

They ran straight back to the Gingerbread Boy's house. And when they got inside, they locked the doors and the windows as fast as they could--but even faster. Then they sat down on the colorful gummy-bear couch to talk about what happened.

The Gingerbread Boy asked, "Why couldn't the Fox eat me? Does anybody know why? Each time he tried, he sneezed very hard."

The oldest pig thought for a minute and then said, "Maybe the Fox is allergic to you."

The middle pig said,

"Gesundheit! You might be right.

The Fox was sneezing left and right.

He seemed to sneeze with all his might.

Oh, NO! Are we wrong?"

[Group says] Or are we right?

[Group says] We might be a snack tonight!

The Gingerbread Boy said, "I have an idea." They huddled in to listen, when suddenly, they heard a knock on the door. Or was it two knocks?

"Who is it?" shouted the oldest pig, fearing the worst, as they all braced themselves against the front door.

Sketch by Philip Costa - Colored by Elle's little brother,
David Dubois III at age four and a half.

7

The Secret

A louder knock came. "Who is it?" shouted the Gingerbread Boy.

"It's us," said the old woman and the old man with the squiggly-wiggly hair and the blue tongue. And at their side was Spotty, the Giraffe with the magic glasses.

"We have a secret song to sing. Let us in and we'll all be safe."

Everyone at the door then sang together:

Catch us if you can,

Bite us if you dare

Our clothes have special pockets

With gingerbread everywhere

One bite and a sneezing Fox you'll be

With a face completely red

And our stoves are warm and loaded

Cooking tasty gingerbread

So please don't come after us,

It won't be good for you

Go on and be a good Fox,

That's a better thing to do.

8

Allergies Can Be Good

The secret the old couple were keeping was that the Fox was allergic to gingerbread, which the Fox found out when he tried to eat the Gingerbread Boy. And the Gingerbread Boy was never really in danger after all. Instead, the Fox's allergies saved the Three Little Pigs! Maybe allergies aren't such a bad thing after all.

The End....

Well, it's really not.

Spotty, the magic Giraffe and Elle

Have more stories to share.

Appendix A

Author Biographies

Elle Valentina Dubois – Elle Dubois, from a small town in Massachusetts, is a typical girl who enjoys swimming, nature, animals, crafts, and of course bossing around her younger brother. At nine months, Elle quickly proved her understanding of the power of language, blurting out her first full sentence: "I want MOMMY!" She has loved stories since she first heard "Once upon a time." From there it's been an exciting adventure in listening and writing for this aspiring author and 2nd -grader. *The Fox Who Sneezed* is her second book; the first book she wrote was about candy, when she was four years old. Here is her first book in its entirety (complete with a picture of Timmy the cat – and addressed to her mom, Michelle). The book was five pages, because we made each sentence one page. And we received copyright permission from Timmy the cat to use him on the cover.

Dear Mommy – I love you and I would like to see you dating and kissing Daddy. I like candy but Grampa says it's bad for you. I like my dog (Stoli), and I love my Grammy. I don't like brussels sprouts. My brother David is 1-year old. He likes chocolate and is mischievous. The End

This "book" took a couple of hours to write with Elle. She insisted on everything that is in her first book. We recommend that everyone sit down and just write down a few sentences to start making their own books, and to learn how to use the power of language. We attribute Elle's extraordinary interest in language to our family story-reading and storytelling almost every day since she was born.

Grampa Steve Kelley - Grampa Steve is an avid storyteller, and Senior Professor at Cambridge College, MA where he teaches Entrepreneurship, Negotiation, Conflict Management, and Leadership. Steve has taught Storytelling, Negotiation, and Classroom Discipline for Teachers at the National Invitation for Teacher Excellence. He has also taught Conflict Management and Effective Listening at Curry College, MA. Steve also owns and manages a real estate management company with his two sons, Dave and Phil. Living in an in-law apartment next to Elle and her family has been key to writing and developing Elle's love of story.

Sarah Feragen - (*Illustrator*) - Sarah is an illustrator, story lover, and art teacher. After receiving a Bachelor of Fine Arts at Mass College of Art and Design, Sarah has honed her skills professionally for four decades and enjoys every opportunity to bring a child's imagination to life. She has also shown her work professionally at the Boston Museum of Science.

Appendix B

Additional Notes on the Development and Writing of the Book

We know the book isn't perfect, and wish for your indulgence in the form, context, transitions, or plot, or any other of the deficiencies one might find. By not eliminating all of the deficiencies, we purposely have written to be true to the creation of the book by a five-year-old. As we mentioned, five-year-old Elle begins the book by telling the story to Grampa, and thinking about the plot, setting, and characters. As she talked more and grew accustomed to her own creation, she grew comfortable with changing the direction of the book.

The Fox Who Sneezed exceeded the expectations of building her confidence, stretching her imagination, and learning how to organize thoughts. Elle originally devised a scheme whereby there were two Gingerbread houses (a fake one in which the Fox lives), and a real one in which the Gingerbread Boy lives. Later as we worked on the book, she decided that the Gingerbread Boy could be protected from the Fox because of the special secret in his body, which nobody knew; the Fox was allergic to gingerbread. It was fun to draw out this incredible story from her. And at one point, Elle said, "The Fox will eat the three pigs, but when the Gingerbread Boy comes close to the Fox, the Fox will sneeze out the three pigs. And they will run away."

Note that in the story, Elle was thinking that kids could be safer in the forest by just having gingerbread in their pockets--so that's part of the ending. As those parts were written, we changed again and again. As we wrote, and realized what a nice project it was, we asked Sarah and Phil for some sketches. We

then decided to look into self-publishing and found the cooperative spirit of Jamie Belt to help us. The book is beautiful, and we are thankful to have set Elle on a path of understanding what she can accomplish with hard work.

We also focused on mistakes, which every child makes, and like adults, tries to explain away their responsibility by calling them accidents. What child hasn't made an "accidental mistake"? It was our hope that this simple heading would draw children deeper into the story.

Equally interesting, the Gingerbread Boy has never really been in danger (he is made of gingerbread, after all) but always thought he was in danger. And a child who carries the "magic" gingerbread can be safe. We asked toward the end, "What are gingerbread, the Fox, and the night-time witch symbols of?"

We also read the book to Elle's little brother David, who contributed several lines. In reading to him, we realized some of our transitions weren't that good. He helped us do better. And he colored one Fox, too.

And just before sending the book off to the publisher, Grammy Susan, who is an excellent proofreader, showed us all of the little mistakes we made--things like using capitals on "Fox" in one place, and "fox" in another. We did that forty-six times. Yikes.

By the end of our writing, Elle was seven, the story had morphed into new ideas, and we decided to change the title from *The Big Bad Forest* to *The Fox Who Sneezed*.

Additionally, the book took on new meaning with multiple purposes. In the beginning we intended simply to build Elle's confidence, and to share Elle's imaginative style with others. By mid-book, we realized that we had a message to share (allergies can be good). And by the end of the book, we felt that we were writing a somewhat participatory book for children. And finally, we wrote the background of the book so that families could see how we did it, in the hopes that they might write a family book too.

We hope that you succeed, and that we did, too!

Elle and Grampa Steve working on their book.